Anxiety Workbook for Kids

ANXIETY
WORKBOOK for KIDS

50+ Fun Mindfulness Activities to Feel Calm, Build Awareness, and Be Your Best Self

AMY NASAMRAN, PhD

callisto
publishing
an imprint of Sourcebooks

To the amazing kids and families who have opened their lives up to me, trusted me, and continue to inspire my work every day.

Published by Callisto Publishing LLC C/O Sourcebooks LLC
P.O. Box 4410, Naperville, Illinois 60567-4410
(630) 961-3900
callistopublishing.com

This product conforms to all applicable CPSC and CPSIA standards.

Source of Production: Wing King Tong Paper Products Co.Ltd. Shenzhen, Guangdong Province, China
Date of Production: October 2023
Run Number: 5035367

Printed and bound in China
WKT 2

CONTENTS

· ·

A LETTER TO GROWN-UPS viii

A LETTER TO KIDS ix

Chapter One: Understanding Anxiety 1

What Is Anxiety? 2

Anxiety Is Your Alarm System 4

What Makes You Anxious? 6

How Anxiety Feels in the Body 9

How Anxiety Affects Thoughts and Feelings 11

Different Kinds of Anxiety 13

Using Your Strengths 15

What Guides You? 17

What You've Learned 19

Chapter Two: The Power of Mindfulness 21

What Is Mindfulness? 22

Mindfulness Magic 25

Mindfulness for Anxiety 27

The Mind-Body Connection 29

Mindful Awareness: Noticing, Not Judging 31

Mindful Attention: Focusing on the Present Moment 34

Mindful Attitude: Being a Beginner 37

Having Fun 39

What You've Learned 41

Chapter Three: Conquering Worry 43

Mindfully Thinking 44

No Judgment 47

Telling Stories 49

Changing Your Thoughts 53

Responding to Your Worries 55

Talking to Yourself Like a Friend 60

Growth Mindset 62

What You've Learned 64

Chapter Four: Focusing on Feelings 67

Mindfully Feeling 68

No Judgment 70

Being Friends with Your Feelings 72

Where Did This Emotion Come From? 75

Let It Out 77

Responding to Your Feelings 79

Finding the Good 83

What You've Learned 85

Chapter Five: The Breath and the Body 87

Mindfully Being 88

Using Your Breath 91

Staying Calm 93

Panic Attacks 95

Responding to Stress 97

Tips for a Healthy Body 101

Self-Care 103

What You've Learned 105

Chapter Six: Taking Action 107

Mindfully Acting 108

Saying "Yes"! 110

Participating in Your Life 112

Connecting with Others 117

Being Kind 119

Asking for Help 121

Confident You! 123

What You've Learned 125

MORE TO LEARN 127

INDEX 129

A LETTER TO
GROWN-UPS

· ·

Welcome, parents, therapists, educators, and other trusted adults.
Children today are experiencing high levels of stress and anxiety. Thank you for choosing this book as one of the resources to help the child or children in your life.

As a psychologist, I'm dedicated to helping children succeed and giving parents and other adults the right tools to help them. Mindfulness is an effective way for kids to learn important skills of attention, emotion regulation, and self-compassion in order to reduce anxiety and improve quality of life. I've personally seen the benefits of mindfulness in my own life and in the well-being of the kids and families with whom I work.

This workbook has 55 activities to help kids ages 8 to 12 learn to use mindfulness to manage everyday stress and anxiety. I invite you to join them in the learning process. The best way to teach children to be mindful is to practice with them. Your positive support and proactive participation will be invaluable in helping them learn coping skills, which we hope will become healthy lifelong habits.

This book is not meant to be a quick fix or substitute for therapy, medication, or professional support. You may realize that more structured support is needed for the child about whom you care deeply. If so, working with a mental health professional may be an important next step.

I hope this book will kick-start your conversations with children about mental health and ongoing mindfulness practice.

A LETTER TO
KImport D S

• •

Hi! Welcome to your new mindfulness workbook. If you sometimes feel nervous or anxious, this book can help. Mindfulness is a way of being aware of the current moment and your feelings, and it can help with anxiety. You'll find many fun activities to help you learn how to handle your anxious thoughts and feelings.

My name is Amy. When I was growing up, many things made me nervous. I was afraid of big dogs. I did *not* like being called on in class. I loved playing sports and the piano but was too nervous to play in front of people. Today, I help other kids brave their fears so they can be their best selves. (And I have a big dog now!)

This book is yours. You can do the activities at your own pace. It's best to practice mindfulness a little bit each day, so keep this book handy.

Have fun! You can write in this book, draw in it, and bookmark your favorite pages. Add your favorite activities to your "mindfulness toolbox" to use anywhere, anytime. Find even more helpful resources on page 127.

If you get stuck, you can always ask an adult for help. It might be fun to do some of the activities together. You definitely don't have to do them by yourself.

Ready to begin learning new skills? I'm so excited for you to get started!

CHAPTER ONE

Understanding Anxiety

Welcome to your first day of mindfulness! In this chapter you'll learn what anxiety is, why it exists, and how to recognize it. Understanding what anxiety is will help you know how to handle it.

WHAT IS ANXIETY?

You may have heard the words *worry*, *stress*, and *anxiety* before. Sometimes people use these words without knowing their actual meanings. Here's what they mean:

WORRY is an emotion. It describes feelings of nervousness or fear. When you feel worried, your mind is thinking something bad might happen.

STRESS is a physical feeling in your body, like feeling tense or stiff, or having a fast-beating heart.

ANXIETY is the emotion of worry plus the physical feeling of stress.

Everyone feels anxiety from time to time. People can feel it during a scary situation, and some feel it even after the situation ends. Take Alex and Henry. Both are scared of thunder. Alex's anxiety passes as soon as a storm is over, but Henry's anxiety remains before and after a storm.

When people feel anxiety in many situations throughout the day, it can start to get in the way of enjoying life. They may be unable to do the things they need or want to do. Take Hannah. She loves hanging out with her friends, but she feels anxious about sleeping away from home. When invited to a sleepover, she avoids going and misses out on time with her friends.

If anxiety has been getting in your way, you're not alone. Using this workbook will teach you tools that can help you feel better.

MEASURING MY ANXIETY

A feelings thermometer can help you measure how much anxiety you feel in different situations. The higher the number on your thermometer, the stronger your anxiety.

On a scale from 1 (least) to 10 (most), Alex might rate her anxiety about thunder a 2 because it quickly goes away, whereas Henry might rate his a 6 because it remains even after storms pass. Hannah might rate her anxiety about sleepovers a 9 or 10 because it stops her from spending time with friends.

Let's identify situations that cause you to have anxiety in your life. Complete the following sentences, then fill in the thermometer to show your level of anxiety for each situation.

I feel a **LITTLE** anxiety about _____

_____

_____

_____

I feel **SOME** anxiety about _____

_____

_____

_____

I feel a **LOT** of anxiety about _____

_____

_____

_____

ANXIETY IS YOUR ALARM SYSTEM

If anxiety feels so bad, we should just get rid of it, right?

But wait! Did you know that anxiety is your brain's way of protecting you from harm?

Anxiety's job is to warn you of danger, so you wouldn't want to get rid of it entirely. When your brain thinks danger is near, it acts like a fire alarm—sending a signal to your body to be careful and prepare for action. This "fight-flight-or-freeze" response is important for survival. All animals, including humans, have it.

In some situations, anxiety can be helpful—for example, when it warns you to stop and look both ways before crossing the street. Some anxiety can help you to study enough to do well on a test or practice enough before a big game.

But anxiety can sometimes ring in a false alarm—it goes off when nothing dangerous is happening. It can even ring for no reason at all.

FINDING FALSE ALARMS

Sometimes your brain can't quite tell how dangerous a situation is. It might think giving a presentation at school and finding a rattlesnake in the classroom are equally dangerous. When you experience false alarms often, anxiety can start to get in your way.

Good news! You can learn how to fine-tune your alarm system. Here's a quiz to help you practice detecting false alarms. (Do your best. It won't be graded.) Decide whether each of the following situations represents a false alarm or a real danger, then circle your choice.

1. **You call someone the wrong name.**

   False alarm   Real danger

2. **Something burning in the oven starts a fire in the kitchen.**

   False alarm   Real danger

3. **When hiking with friends, you see a bear off in the distance.**

   False alarm   Real danger

4. **When you get to school, you realize you left your homework at home.**

   False alarm   Real danger

5. **You see a burglar breaking into a neighbor's house.**

   False alarm   Real danger

6. **At the park, some kids you don't know invite you to join them in a game.**

   False alarm   Real danger

Answers: 1. False alarm   2. Real danger   3. Real danger   4. False alarm   5. Real danger   6. False alarm

WHAT MAKES YOU ANXIOUS?

Scientists think anxiety may have several causes. It might come from biology (how your brain and body are made), personal experiences, or events in the world—such as scary things in the news. It might be caused by a combination of these things.

Things that cause anxiety to arise are called *triggers*. Places, people, activities, or life situations can trigger anxiety. Here are some examples:

PLACES

→ School

→ Doctor's office

→ Places you've never been before

PEOPLE

→ Kids or adults you don't know well

→ Certain classmates

→ Authority figures, such as school principals, coaches, or police

ACTIVITIES

→ Doing homework or taking tests

→ Doing something for the first time

→ Sleeping away from home

LIFE SITUATIONS

→ Moving to a new home or going to a new school

→ Getting sick

→ Getting a new sibling

Not all people have the same triggers. Some people are scared of heights, for example, and riding roller coasters would be their trigger. Others aren't afraid of heights and think roller coasters are fun.

Figuring out what makes you feel anxious is a big part of learning what you can do to help yourself feel better.

LEARNING MY ANXIETY TRIGGERS

Let's learn more about your anxiety triggers. Make a list of places, people, activities, and life situations that cause you to worry.

PLACES That Make Me Anxious:	**PEOPLE** Who Make Me Anxious:
-------------------------------	-------------------------------
-------------------------------	-------------------------------
-------------------------------	-------------------------------
-------------------------------	-------------------------------
ACTIVITIES That Make Me Anxious:	**LIFE SITUATIONS** That Made or Make Me Anxious:
-------------------------------	-------------------------------
-------------------------------	-------------------------------
-------------------------------	-------------------------------
-------------------------------	-------------------------------

Write down anything else that makes you feel worried:

HOW ANXIETY FEELS IN THE BODY

Remember, anxiety is like a built-in alarm system. When your brain thinks danger is nearby, it sends a signal to your body. This alarm sets off a "fight-flight-or-freeze" response. Depending on whether your response is to fight the danger, run and hide, or shut down, you might experience:

→ Butterflies in your stomach or a stomachache

→ Dizziness or a headache

→ Dry mouth

→ Short and fast breaths as though you just ran a sprint

→ Fast heartbeats

→ Muscles tightening

→ Sweatiness

→ Shaky or fidgety hands, arms, or legs

→ Trouble falling asleep

→ Don't want to (or can't) eat

All animals can have these reactions. (Have you ever seen a dog's hair sticking up on its back when it's scared?) They're part of our biology.

Even though the body's reactions to anxiety are totally normal, they can be uncomfortable and cause worry. For example, you might be a great reader but fear that others can hear your voice shaking when you read aloud. The good news is that your body is totally capable of calming itself.

ACTIVITY 4

FEELING THE FEELINGS

It can be hard to imagine how your body will react when you experience anxiety, especially if you're not feeling anxious right now. It can take some practice to really notice how your body reacts when anxiety arises.

Use this exercise to create and take note of different physical feelings that you may or may not experience when you feel anxious.

TRY THIS MOVE	NOTICE THE FEELING	DO YOU NOTICE THIS FEELING WHEN YOU ARE ANXIOUS?
Do 25 jumping jacks or arm jacks (bend your elbows and pump your arms up toward the ceiling and back down).	Do you feel your heart beating faster? YES NO	YES NO
Turn around 10 times on your feet or in a swivel chair.	Do you feel your head spinning? YES NO	YES NO
Make a fist and squeeze it for 20 seconds.	Do you feel your muscles tightening? YES NO	YES NO
Quickly blow up a balloon (if you don't have a balloon, hold your breath for 20 seconds).	Do you feel out of breath? YES NO	YES NO

Later in this book, we'll practice some ways to help calm the physical feelings of anxiety.

HOW ANXIETY AFFECTS THOUGHTS AND FEELINGS

Anxiety causes you to go into high alert, which affects the way you think and feel.

When you're on the lookout for danger, your thoughts may become more negative than usual. You might lose sight of anything else that's happening and focus only on your worries.

Anxiety can also cause you to feel other tough emotions. You might begin to doubt yourself and think you can't do things that other kids can do. You might feel frustrated, angry, or down on yourself. These emotions can lead to even more problems, like missing out on activities.

Anxiety can negatively affect your thoughts and feelings by:

→ Making you assume the worst will happen

→ Focusing your attention on the negative possibilities instead of the positive ones

→ Causing you to doubt yourself or compare yourself to others

→ Making you sensitive to or bothered by sounds around you

→ Making you avoid places, people, or activities you might have found enjoyable

ACTIVITY 5

BURSTING ANXIOUS THOUGHT BUBBLES

Imagine you're a cartoon or comic book character, and your thoughts appear in bubbles above you. Now that you know anxiety increases negative thoughts, you can start to burst the bubbles that contain those thoughts.

When was a recent time you were anxious? In the box provided, draw yourself in that scene. Add thought bubbles and write in your anxious thoughts. Then imagine yourself bursting those thought bubbles.

DIFFERENT KINDS OF ANXIETY

As we've learned, anxiety can have many triggers and take different forms.
Some people feel anxious in general. Their false alarm goes off all day long—when they're trying to get to places on time, doing things at school, and even trying to relax at home. Other people feel anxious at specific times—for example, when they're around others—or about specific things, like certain animals or events.

Anxiety can involve being away from caregivers, family members, or trusted adults. That worry might be caused by the thought that something bad might happen if you are separated for too long.

Some anxiety involves a recurring thought and action. When people have an anxious thought that keeps popping up, they might try to make it stop with a certain behavior, such as touching or tapping things, or counting to themselves.

NAMING YOUR ANXIETY

Now that you know the different kinds of anxiety, which ones do you relate to the most? Do you feel anxious about a specific topic, or does your anxiety feel like it's there in general throughout the day? Maybe you feel anxious when speaking or doing things in front of other people. Or maybe your anxiety is a combination of a few types of anxiety.

Once you understand what your anxiety is like, give it a name. For example, you could name your anxiety "The Worry Bully" if it tries to boss you around all day. Or "Stormy" if you worry specifically about bad weather.

Naming your anxiety can help you notice it. You can say to yourself, "There's Stormy again." Noticing when your anxiety shows up can help you decide what to do to help calm it down instead of letting it take over. Let's try naming your anxiety now.

My anxiety's name is _.

Draw a picture of what your anxiety might look like. Would it have a face like a human or be more like an animal or cartoon character? Maybe it looks like an item or an object. Is it big or small? What color is it? Include its features in your drawing.

USING YOUR STRENGTHS

When anxiety takes over a situation, you might feel scared and powerless—like you want to run away or give up. Anxiety can make you forget about the qualities that make you unique and awesome.

You are more than your fears and anxiety. You are good at and enjoy doing some things! You can use your strengths to help yourself get through stressful situations.

Let's say you moved to a new school and are feeling nervous about making new friends or fitting in with the other kids. You can remind yourself of the qualities that make you a good friend, like being kind, funny, or always willing to help others. Thinking about these qualities will help you feel more confident about meeting new people. In fact, it can help you feel more confident about yourself all the time.

Remember the times you've tried new or hard things? Maybe you practiced and got better at something that was once a challenge to do. Remembering your accomplishments can help you keep going and find even more success.

The fact that you're reading this book means you're open to learning new things. That's a strength! This book will teach you many new skills that you can turn into even more strengths.

Next Time . . .

Last night I watched a scary movie and couldn't fall asleep. I was afraid to sleep in my bed alone. I kept worrying that something bad might happen to me or my family. Next time, I'll remember that I'm brave for all the nights I've slept in my own room and remind myself that my house is safe.

REMEMBERING MY SUPERPOWERS

All the things that make you special and unique are easy to forget when anxiety takes over. It's important to remember your strengths so you can use them when things get tough.

Start thinking about your strengths by filling in the blanks below.

My favorite subject, or something I'm good at, is _

Something I have fun doing, even if I'm not the best at it, is _ _ _ _ _ _ _ _ _ _ _ _ _ _ _ _ _ _ _

_ _

One thing my friends like about me is _

My teacher would say I'm good at _

Something nice I've done for someone else was _

_ _

I'm happiest when _

My family would say I'm good at _

One thing that makes me unique is _

_ _

Something I accomplished today is _

_ _

One thing I'm proud of myself for is _

_ _

WHAT GUIDES YOU?

Have you ever heard of the North Star? It is the brightest star in the sky. For thousands of years, sailors and explorers used it to point them in the right direction, especially during strong winds and rough seas.

Many people have their own guiding stars for setting and accomplishing goals. These guiding stars are the things that matter to them.

Knowing what's important to you can help you set goals and do things that feel hard. For example, if eating healthy food matters to you, you might set a goal to eat vegetables, even if they're not your favorite foods. If your friends matter to you, you might set a goal to go out on the playground with them at recess instead of staying in the classroom, even when you feel anxious about the older kids being mean. If soccer matters to you, you might set a goal to play every game, even if you're worried about missing free kicks or playing in front of a crowd.

Just as the North Star guided sailors on their tough journeys, the things that matter to you will help steer you in the right direction, even when you feel anxious.

CHOOSING MY GUIDING STARS

Now that you've listed some of your pretty amazing strengths and powers, it's time to choose your guiding stars and set some goals.

Draw three large stars on a piece of construction paper. On each, write one thing—maybe learning about robotics or trying out for a play—that's important to you or a goal you'd like to work toward. Decorate the stars, then cut them out and tape them up where you can see them every day. They will remind you of what you value and the goals you're working toward.

WHAT YOU'VE LEARNED

In this chapter, you learned that anxiety is your body's alarm system. You found out about the ways anxiety affects your thoughts and feelings and the different forms it takes. Finally, you identified some of your superpowers and guiding stars.

You're now ready to learn tools for mindfulness. You'll use these tools to help yourself feel better whenever anxiety shows up.

In this chapter, I learned:

Learning this information is helpful because:

So far, the most helpful idea or exercise for me is:

CHAPTER TWO

The Power of Mindfulness

Now that you know more about anxiety, are you ready to learn about mindfulness and how it can help calm anxiety? In this chapter, you will discover tools for mindfulness and fun ways to practice it.

WHAT IS MINDFULNESS?

Mindfulness is a special way of paying attention to yourself and what's going on in the present moment.

You have probably been mindful without realizing it. If you've ever put together a puzzle, you paid close attention to the colors, shapes, and sizes of its pieces. You noticed how they fit together as you carefully put them in place. You weren't thinking about anything but the task in front of you. That total focus on the present is being mindful.

Sometimes people picture mindfulness as sitting cross-legged and meditating with their eyes closed. But mindfulness isn't just about meditating or clearing your mind. It's about learning how to focus your attention. You notice when you get distracted by the past or the future and bring your focus back to what's happening in the present—like shining a spotlight on yourself in the exact moment you're living.

Mindfulness can be a powerful tool for managing anxiety. You can use it to notice what's happening around you when anxiety arises, for example: what your mind is thinking, how your body is feeling, and what you're doing. When you take the time to be aware of your body, thoughts, feelings, and actions, you can prevent anxiety from taking over.

Take Anderson, who was nervous about going to the dentist. On the way there, he focused his attention on himself and what was happening in the present moment. He noticed his body tensing and his heart beating fast. Paying attention to what was happening in the moment helped him catch and calm his anxious feelings before they grew too big to manage.

START WITH A SNACK

This activity will help you start learning what it's like to mindfully shift your attention to the present moment as it's happening.

Pretend you've been given a special mission to teach a robot about a snack that humans enjoy. The robot needs to know information in detail. To begin, choose a snack that you have at home—cookies, raisins, orange slices, popcorn, or any small piece of food. Now describe it to your robot.

What does it look like? What color and shape does it have?

What does it smell like?

What texture does it have and how much does it weigh?

----

continued→

Start with a Snack, *continued*

What sounds do you hear as you chew it?

How does it taste?

What does it feel like in your mouth?

Were you able to focus and perhaps notice something new about the snack? Or did you catch your mind wandering and thinking about something else altogether?

MINDFULNESS MAGIC

Mindfulness is so important that it is taught in schools all over the world. It has helped students concentrate and perform better on tests. It has made them feel less anxious and act more kindly toward one another.

Mindfulness can help you:

→ Pay better attention

→ Focus

→ Feel less angry, scared, sad, and stressed

→ Be brave and more confident

→ Feel calm

→ Understand your emotions and how to manage them

→ Learn more about yourself

→ Be kinder to yourself and others

→ Sleep better

Kids who practice mindfulness can use it to handle tough situations at home, at school, and out in the world. They find it easier to bounce back from setbacks because they can keep their emotions from getting in the way of doing what's important to them—like being a good friend, learning something new, or playing sports or musical instruments.

PLAY A MINDFUL MEMORY GAME

Mindfulness helps you slow down, pay attention, and gather more information to make good decisions instead of reacting to your thoughts and emotions. Ready to see it in action?

You'll need a timer and something to draw with for this activity. Pick a nearby window. Give yourself five seconds to look out of it. Then, turn around. Draw in the box below as many things that you can remember seeing, without looking again.

Next, look out the same window, and this time give yourself 30 seconds to observe. Turn around and draw again what you saw, adding any new details. I bet you remembered much more this time.

Slowing down to observe the present moment can give you more—and better—information about your surroundings.

MINDFULNESS FOR ANXIETY

Mindfulness can be extra helpful for coping with strong emotions like anxiety. Coping means using skills to manage tough emotions so they do not overwhelm you.

Anxiety can make it hard for you to do what you need to do. You might become overwhelmed by your body's physical responses or your mind's worries and act in unhelpful ways.

Mindfulness can help you pay attention and notice your thoughts, feelings, and surroundings when anxiety shows up. With mindfulness, you can help yourself feel better before anxiety takes over.

Mindfulness can help you manage anxiety so you can:

→ Notice and calm your body's physical reactions before you feel too overwhelmed

→ Understand what causes or triggers your anxiety

→ Focus on things as they're happening rather than worrying about the past or future

→ Look at situations more clearly so you can make better decisions

→ Stop your emotions from running the show

USE YOUR FIVE SENSES

Grounding exercises help you focus on the present moment by turning your attention from anxious thoughts to what's happening in the here and now. One way to refocus your attention is to practice using your five senses: hearing, smell, sight, taste, and touch. Observing your senses can tell you a lot about what's happening right here, right now.

This grounding exercise can be done anywhere, including in your home or outside.

1. **Plant your feet on the ground right where you are, or find a comfortable place to sit.**

2. **Using your sense of sight, notice five things you can see around you.**

3. **Using your sense of touch, notice four things you can feel on your body.**

4. **Using your sense of hearing, listen closely for three sounds.**

5. **Using your sense of smell, notice two things you can smell.**

6. **Using your sense of taste, notice one thing you can taste. (If you're in a situation where you can't taste anything, notice one positive thought.)**

How did you feel after doing this activity? Did you feel any different after focusing your attention on the present moment? Did you notice any changes to your body—for example, changes in your heart rate or posture?

THE MIND-BODY CONNECTION

You may already know that our minds and bodies are connected. But what exactly does this mean?

The mind-body connection is how your mind and body work together. Your thoughts can affect the way your body reacts, and your body can affect your mind's thoughts and feelings.

If you wake up and your mind thinks, "I can't wait to see my friends today!" you might feel happy and excited. Your body might feel energized. When you get to school, you might run quickly onto the playground to see your friends.

But if your mind thinks, "I don't want to go to recess today. I never know who to play with," you might feel nervous. Your body might tense up or shake. When it's time for recess, you might avoid going outside. Your mind changed your body.

The opposite can also happen. Your body's physical reactions can affect your thoughts and emotions. For example, you might know the answer to a question your teacher asks you in class. But then your palms start sweating, and you don't raise your hand. In that case, your body changed your mind.

Understanding how your thoughts, emotions, and body are linked can help you choose the right mindfulness tools when anxiety shows up.

TRY DEEP BREATHING

Deep breathing can help calm your brain and body. Remember how your brain sends a signal to your body when it thinks danger is near? In fight-flight-or-freeze mode, your breathing becomes short, fast, and shallow.

Slowing your breath can send the reverse signal to your brain. It will let your brain know that everything is okay. When you take slower, longer, and bigger breaths, your heart rate goes down. A slower heart rate tells your brain that you're not actually in any danger. Your brain's alarm stops going off. You can start to feel calmer and more relaxed.

Let's practice some deep breathing.

1. **Take a deep breath in through your nose. Count in your head to four.**

2. **Exhale through your mouth. Count silently to eight.**

3. **Repeat this exercise four or five times.**

Easy!

How do you feel after doing the exercise?

- -

- -

- -

MINDFUL AWARENESS: NOTICING, NOT JUDGING

Mindfulness teaches your mind to notice things in a new way. Mindful awareness means observing something without judging it. Judging something is having an opinion about it. Typically, you decide whether you like or don't like something or if it's good or bad. Everyone has things they like and don't like. Your mind makes judgments about things all day long—whether you like what you're eating, whether it's too hot or too cold outside, whether an activity is fun or boring. Judgments about whether situations are safe or dangerous can be helpful.

But sometimes, judgments can make life harder for you. Fighting for things you like and against things you don't can become a constant struggle. When anxiety shows up, judgments can be wrong (like a false anxiety alarm). They might even be harmful. When your mind makes judgments like "This is impossible" or "I'm not good at this," you might give up on, avoid, or miss out on things that matter to you.

When you learn to notice instead of judge, you can see the facts of a situation more clearly. Imagine the observing part of your mind like a magnifying glass. Looking closely at a situation, it notices what it observes, without giving an opinion. If you mindfully observe instead of judge, you can make decisions without anxious thoughts and feelings getting in your way.

continued→

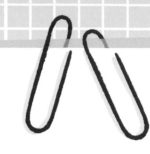

Mindful Awareness: Noticing, Not Judging, *continued*

> **Next Time . . .**
>
> *Yesterday I was nervous about riding the bus to school. My mind made judgments like "The kids on the bus are too loud" and "Being on the bus is not fun, so I can't do it." Next time, I'll notice my judging thoughts and try to focus only on facts, such as "The bus takes me to school."*

PULL OUT YOUR MIND'S MAGNIFYING GLASS

Not judging things can take some practice because your mind wants to judge. Practice using your mind's magnifying glass. Remember that its job is to closely observe and be aware of things just as they are, noting only facts.

SITUATION	OBSERVE THE FACTS	NOTICE YOUR JUDGMENTS
Using a thermometer or a weather app, step outside and jot down the temperature.	It is - - - - - - - - - degrees outside.	Did your mind make any judgments, such as it's too hot or too cold? **YES NO**
Count the pillows on your bed.	There are - - - - - - - - - pillows on my bed.	Did your mind make any judgments, such as liking or disliking your bed? **YES NO**
Find a staircase and count its steps.	There are - - - - - - - - - steps. The steps are made of - - - - - - - - -	Did your mind make any judgments, such as the staircase is too long? **YES NO**

MINDFUL ATTENTION: FOCUSING ON THE PRESENT MOMENT

Mindfulness is about learning to focus on the present moment. Paying mindful attention to the present moment is different from being on autopilot—that is, going about your day without paying attention to what you're doing, like your mind is switched off.

When you're nervous or anxious, it can be extra hard to focus on the present. Your mind might tell you to run and hide. It might wander off and worry about past mistakes or the future.

But when you're paying mindful attention and focusing on the present moment, you can live your life how you want—as it's happening. Paying attention in this special way helps you become more aware of your thoughts and feelings, and what's happening in front of you.

Living in the present moment can help you see more possibilities. You can make better decisions about what you want. You can think about what's important without letting automatic or anxious thinking get in the way. When your attention is on the present instead of switched off or focused on the past or future, you might even notice new, interesting, and fun aspects of your life.

WATCH A MOVIE OF YOUR LIFE

One way to practice paying attention to the present is to imagine that you're watching a movie about your life as it's happening.

Give your life movie a title. _____

Who would play you? _____

Shine the spotlight on yourself in this very moment. Draw a scene of yourself and include details about what you look like, where you are, and what you're doing.

continued →

Watch a Movie of Your Life, *continued*

Reflect on this activity: While drawing your scene, did you notice anything about yourself or your surroundings that you didn't notice earlier?

Did you catch your mind wandering off, wondering about the future or thinking about something that happened yesterday? Were you able to bring your focus back to your present moment? What strategies did you use?

MINDFUL ATTITUDE: BEING A BEGINNER

Do you remember what it's like to be a beginner at something? Maybe you remember learning how to ride a bike. Learning a new activity isn't always easy. Taking off the training wheels might have felt scary at first, even if you ride perfectly now.

Mindfulness is being comfortable with being a beginner in any situation in your life, especially when the situation is hard or makes you feel anxious.

A beginner's attitude lets you try new things without expecting to be good or perfect at them. It means you understand that making mistakes is totally normal when doing or learning something new. Everyone has times when things don't go well or turn out how they expected. If you have a beginner's attitude, you treat yourself kindly when you make mistakes. You're curious about learning how to do better next time.

Having a beginner's attitude is especially important when it comes to coping with anxiety. It can be hard to treat yourself kindly when anxiety shows up. Your mind might say mean things, such as "What's wrong with me?" or "I can't do this." But with a beginner's attitude, you can give yourself the encouragement you deserve to face anxiety and figure out new ways to keep learning and to overcome setbacks and challenges.

ANXIOUS ATTITUDE OR BEGINNER'S ATTITUDE?

Getting comfortable with being a beginner can take some practice. Can you tell which of the following thoughts reflect a beginner's attitude and which reflect an anxious attitude? Write an "A" next to the thoughts that suggest an anxious attitude. Write a "B" next to the ones that suggest a beginner's attitude. Remember, it's okay to be a beginner here—you won't be graded!

1. **"I'm the worst violinist in the orchestra."** _____ ☐

2. **"I'm not the best player on the team, but if I practice, I can improve my serve."** _____ ☐

3. **"There's no way I'll study everything in time to pass my math test tomorrow."** _____ ☐

4. **"Going to new places can be scary for me, but I can try to go for part of the time."** _____ ☐

5. **"I'm not comfortable going on the field trip if I don't know the exact plans."** _____ ☐

6. **"Fractions are hard for me, but I'm still learning."** _____ ☐

Answers: 1. A   2. B   3. A   4. B   5. A   6. B

HAVING FUN

Still getting the hang of mindfulness? That's okay! Mindfulness isn't about "getting it right" or doing things perfectly. As long as you practice and keep an open mind, you're doing great.

Learning mindfulness is just like learning any other new activity—the more you do it, the better you'll get. For example, if you want to learn how to swim, you could watch videos about swimming. A swim coach could explain how to move your arms and kick your feet. But to really learn how to swim, you have to actually get in the pool and practice swimming. The best way to learn mindfulness is to practice it. The activities in this book are a great place to start.

Mindfulness tools are most helpful when you use them regularly. Over time, you'll learn which tools you like best and which ones help you lower your stress and anxiety the most. As you learn how to use them to handle your anxiety, you'll have more time to do things you love, like spending time with friends and family.

DON'T CRY OVER SPILLED . . . WATER

Have you ever heard someone say, "Don't cry over spilled milk"? They mean that even when things don't go your way, you can have a positive attitude. Let's put this idea to use with some fun mindfulness challenges.

CHALLENGE 1: Grab a cup and fill it with water as close to the top as possible without spilling over.

How did you do? Circle the mindfulness strategies you used, then write down any others that you thought of while completing the challenge.

Self-compassion   Deep breathing

Using sight, touch, sound, smell, or taste   Noticing, not judging

Focusing on the present   -
                                                                             Write your own

CHALLENGE 2: With your cup full of water, walk as quickly as you can from one end of the room to the other without spilling any water.

How did you do? Circle the mindfulness strategies you used, then write down any others that you thought of while completing the challenge.

Self-compassion   Deep breathing

Using sight, touch, sound, smell, or taste   Noticing, not judging

Focusing on the present   -
                                                                             Write your own

If any water spilled (it happens!), remember that practicing mindfulness is supposed to be fun. Allow yourself to be silly.

WHAT YOU'VE LEARNED

In this chapter, you learned about mindfulness—what it is and why it's important. You learned how it can help you manage stress and anxiety. Most important, you began your mindfulness practice. This chapter's activities will set you up to add more tools to your mindfulness toolbox.

Take a minute now to write about how you feel after trying mindfulness activities for the first time.

In this chapter, I learned:

Learning this information is helpful because:

So far, the most helpful idea or exercise for me is:

CHAPTER THREE

Conquering Worry

In this chapter, you'll learn how mindfulness can help you recognize your mind's anxious thoughts. You'll practice ways to recognize when your mind worries and understand what it worries about. You'll also learn how to respond to these worries in helpful ways.

MINDFULLY THINKING

How do thoughts affect us? Let's look at an example. While taking a test at school, Emery gets stuck but is nervous about asking her teacher for help. She thinks to herself, "What if the teacher is mean? What if I fail this test?" Emery notices that she's starting to feel anxious and takes a deep breath. She refocuses her attention on the present moment. She notices that her many "what ifs" aren't likely to happen and feels better about asking her teacher for help.

Your thoughts are the things you say to yourself in your head, like:

→ "I love this song!"

→ "I can't wait to eat when I get home."

→ "Why can't I do anything right?"

→ "What was that sound?"

Your mind is always thinking. When one thought passes, another appears. Sometimes, when you're not paying attention, you might believe what you're thinking is actually happening. It's easy to forget that thoughts are just things that your mind is thinking about—they are not facts.

As you learned in chapter 1, your thoughts can affect the way you feel and what you do. Anxiety is when you have many worried thoughts throughout the day, and you get stuck believing that they're true and playing out in real life.

Instead of letting your thoughts stop you from doing what you need or want to do, you can take control by being mindful of them.

I'M HAVING THE THOUGHT THAT . . .

Noticing your thoughts takes practice. One way to start is to say to yourself, "I'm having the thought that . . ." before each thought you have. For example, "I'm having the thought that . . . I'm thirsty. I'm having the thought that . . . I have homework to do. I'm having the thought that . . . I'm ready to try it!"

Even though you can't see your thoughts, imagine them coming and going in thought bubbles above your head—just as you did in the cartoon exercise in chapter 1. Practice noticing the thoughts that pop into your head during an activity you do each day, such as getting dressed, eating dinner, or listening to music. Mindful thinking during everyday activities will help that thinking feel natural when you need to use it during a situation that makes you feel anxious.

Try to notice your thoughts each day for one week. Check off each day that you remember to picture your thought bubbles, and rate how easy or hard it was for you. Tip: It's okay to start this exercise mid-week and continue it for seven days.

SUNDAY	☐ I practiced today! **Noticing my thoughts today was:** ☐ Easy ☐ Sort of hard ☐ Hard
MONDAY	☐ I practiced today! **Noticing my thoughts today was:** ☐ Easy ☐ Sort of hard ☐ Hard
TUESDAY	☐ I practiced today! **Noticing my thoughts today was:** ☐ Easy ☐ Sort of hard ☐ Hard

continued →

I'm Having the Thought That . . ., *continued*

WEDNESDAY	☐ I practiced today! Noticing my thoughts today was: ☐ Easy ☐ Sort of hard ☐ Hard
THURSDAY	☐ I practiced today! Noticing my thoughts today was: ☐ Easy ☐ Sort of hard ☐ Hard
FRIDAY	☐ I practiced today! Noticing my thoughts today was: ☐ Easy ☐ Sort of hard ☐ Hard
SATURDAY	☐ I practiced today! Noticing my thoughts today was: ☐ Easy ☐ Sort of hard ☐ Hard

NO JUDGMENT

Your mind's job is to think, but it doesn't always let you pick what to think about. If you've ever had a thought you didn't like and told yourself, "Just don't think about it," then you know how hard that is to do.

Mindfulness is about letting your mind do its job—to think—and observing all its thoughts, whether you like them or not.

Everyone has worried thoughts from time to time. When you negatively judge these thoughts and try to push them away, you end up struggling more with them. Judging your thoughts gives them the power to get in your way.

Not judging your thoughts means taking a step back to see them for what they are—just words. Looking at your thoughts in this way can help you take away their power to control what you do or affect how you feel.

Here are some tips for noticing your thoughts without judging them:

→ Picture your thoughts as words in bubbles above your head.

→ Remind yourself that words have no power to control or hurt you.

→ Imagine your thoughts are just passing by like clouds in the sky.

Next Time . . .

Yesterday at dance practice, I was nervous about getting on stage. I noticed my mind worrying about being watched and messing up. I tried so hard to not think about messing up that I couldn't focus on my routine. Next time, I'll notice my thoughts. I'll let them pass instead of judging them.

THOUGHT EXPERIMENT

For this exercise, you'll need a ball and a bucket of water. Find a tennis ball, ping-pong ball, or any ball that floats.

Imagine the ball represents your worried thoughts. Push the ball under water and try to make it stay there. It's a struggle to keep the ball down! Without the pressure of your hand pushing the ball down, it will pop up. This is like what happens to your thoughts when you try to push your thoughts down in your mind, and don't engage with them.

Now, release the ball. Imagine you're letting go of your anxious thoughts to rise to the surface, just like the ball. Notice that you're no longer fighting with the thoughts. It takes a lot less work to let them be than to try to push them away. Just like the ball, your thoughts are there, but they can't hurt or control you.

Direct your attention to other things and any people around you right now. Do you notice that you can do something entirely different from what you were doing, even though the ball is still there? You can do what you need or want to do more easily when you're not fighting with thoughts that you don't like.

TELLING STORIES

Your mind puts thoughts together to tell you stories about who you are. It tells you what other people think about you and what might happen in the future. When these stories pop into your mind, it might be easy to believe them. But the stories aren't always accurate. Sometimes they're missing facts. Sometimes they're not true at all.

Anxiety makes your mind focus on the parts of the story that are negative. Your mind looks for evidence that proves its worries are true. It brushes off any information that would allow the worries to stop.

Let's say you're worried about not making a sports team. Your mind might remember all the times you've messed up or lost a game. It will use those times as evidence to strengthen your worry. It will ignore evidence that would lessen your worry, such as how hard you've been practicing and how much encouragement you've received from your coach.

The stories your mind tells you can be very convincing. But listening to a one-sided story could stop you from seeing things clearly. It could lead you to have false beliefs about your life.

Here are some ways to recognize one-sided stories your mind tells:

→ Think about whether the story is overly negative. Did it leave out any positive details?

→ Make a list of evidence that disagrees with the story.

→ Talk to someone you trust. Does that person see things the same way that you do? Do they have any new information to add?

ANXIETY'S TALL TALES

Understanding what kinds of stories your anxious mind tells you can help you begin to change the story. Here are some examples of stories that anxiety likes to tell.

JUMPING TO THE WORST-CASE SCENARIO: Assuming the worst will happen

> "My best friend didn't want to hang out today, so they must not like me or want to be friends anymore."

ALWAYS-OR-NEVER THINKING: Based on one experience, expecting something to always or never be true

> "I messed up at my recital. I'm never going to be good."
> "It's raining on my party day. This always happens to me."

FORGETTING THE GOOD THINGS: Focusing only on what went wrong, or could go wrong, in a situation

> "We lost the basketball game. It doesn't matter if I scored points and my coach said I did a good job."

ASKING TOO MANY WHAT-IFS: Asking many questions about what could happen before a situation even happens

> "I want to go to the birthday party, but what if I'm left out? What if I don't know how to play the games? What if the other kids make fun of me?"

Now write your own examples. Later, in activities 21 and 23, we'll come up with more realistic thoughts to replace these anxious stories.

Jumping to the Worst-Case Scenario:

Always-or-Never Thinking:

Forgetting the Good Things:

Asking Too Many What-Ifs:

Write Your Own Example:

PUTTING YOUR STORY BACK ON THE SHELF

Choose one of your mind's favorite stories to tell and give it a name. For example, the "I Can't Do It" story or the "What If" story. Write your story's title here.

- -

When this story shows up, recognize it by name in your mind. Imagine filing it away like a book you've already read. You don't need to read it again. Let's practice.

1. **Find a quiet place to sit down and close your eyes.**

2. **Imagine the story popping up in your mind or as a book in your hands. You could say, "Oh, it's the 'I Can't Do It' story. I've heard it before."**

3. **Then, imagine yourself placing the story back on the shelf, like a book at the library. Once you've acknowledged it and filed it away, you don't have to read it again. There's no need to give it any more attention.**

4. **Refocus your attention on what you're doing in the present moment. What do you see around you? How is your body moving? What sounds can you hear?**

CHANGING YOUR THOUGHTS

Anxiety can cloud your thinking. It can lead you to false beliefs about yourself or the world around you. It makes you see the world through a negative lens, like you're wearing muddy glasses. When wearing anxiety's negative glasses, your mind looks for anything wrong. It might think about worst-case scenarios. Anxiety tries to make negative details take up all the space around you, blurring out anything positive.

It can be easy to believe everything your thoughts tell you. Negative and anxious thoughts are very strong and convincing but, as you're now learning, thoughts can be changed.

You can change the story, or narrative, by adding coping thoughts to it. We learned in chapter 2 that coping thoughts are neutral and positive ones. You can call them up when your anxious mind is thinking only negative thoughts. Coping thoughts are not just about trying to "be positive"—they also help you notice important and realistic details, giving you a clearer perspective and taking the power away from one-sided, negative thoughts.

Here are some ways to create coping thoughts:

→ Notice and describe the facts of the situation.

→ Try to name the anxious stories that your mind might be telling.

→ Imagine what you would say to a good friend who was anxious and having worries like yours.

COPING THOUGHTS

Let's practice turning one-sided, negative thoughts into helpful coping thoughts. Read some examples, then write some of your own.

TURN UNHELPFUL, NEGATIVE THOUGHTS . . .	. . . INTO HELPFUL COPING THOUGHTS
I messed up my artwork. It's going to be the worst artwork in the class.	My artwork didn't turn out how I wanted, but I've made other good pieces before. I can improve next time.
The coach saw me miss a basket. Now I won't make the team.	The coach saw me miss a basket, but she's also seen me play well before.
I can't go to my doctor's appointment. It's going to be scary!	- -
My friend didn't want to eat lunch with me today. No one at this school likes me.	- -
I'm not going to try out for the talent show. When I mess up, everyone will laugh at me.	- -
- -	- -

RESPONDING TO YOUR WORRIES

E ven though you can't always control the thoughts and worries that pop up in your mind, you have the power to respond to them. With mindfulness, you learn to stop letting your worries control how you feel and what you do.

Without mindfulness, you might believe anything that pops into your head—sometimes without even realizing it. You might believe thoughts that aren't accurate or let your worries convince you to give up or run away.

But when you're mindful, you—not your thoughts—stay in charge. Observing and noticing your thoughts, without letting them control you allows you to be the boss. You can choose to turn down the volume of overly negative or unhelpful thoughts. You can even get one step ahead of them by imagining how you would handle them. Sometimes, the reason thoughts feel scary is because you think you can't handle them. But you can!

Here are some ways to practice mindfully responding to your thoughts:

→ Thank your mind for the thought without doing what it says. For example, think to yourself, "Thank you for telling me. I'll decide what to do."

→ Imagine your mind's thoughts are like a song on a radio, and turn down the volume.

→ Face your thought instead of letting it scare you. Ask yourself, "If this thought is actually true, what can I do to handle it?"

CLOUD-WATCHING AT NIGHT

Sometimes anxious thoughts make it hard to fall or stay asleep. When you can't sleep, look up at the ceiling or close your eyes. Imagine your thoughts are passing by, like clouds in the moonlit sky. Watch them come and go.

Keep responding to anxious nighttime thoughts in this way. You can watch the thoughts float by, and you don't have to let them overpower you. Just like clouds, your thoughts can't hurt you or control what happens.

Inside the clouds below, write some thoughts that pop up in your mind as you're trying to fall asleep. Then pretend you're watching them disappear into the night sky.

SPOT THE COPING THOUGHT

Many kids have anxious thoughts at school. It can be tricky to be mindful when you have a busy schedule and little quiet time to yourself.

This activity will help you practice balancing by using coping thoughts to replace the negative thoughts that tend to creep up at school. Spot the coping thought in each of these situations and circle it.

1. **Taking a hard test**

    a. "This test is so hard. I can't do it."

    b. "I should have studied more. Now I'm going to fail."

    c. "This test is hard, but I've finished hard tests before."

    d. "My parents are going to be so mad at me and take away my privileges."

2. **Making friends**

    a. "Nobody wants to be my partner on this project."

    b. "I don't know Allen very well yet, but he has been nice to me before. I'll ask him to work on the project."

    c. "I'm always picked last because nobody likes me."

    d. "Everyone in class is talking about me and making fun of me."

continued→

Spot the Coping Thought, *continued*

3. **Talking to my teacher**

    a. "If I ask my teacher for help, he'll think I wasn't paying attention."

    b. "If I get called on, I'll give the wrong answer, and everyone will think I'm dumb."

    c. "My teacher doesn't like me as much as she likes the other kids."

    d. "I don't know my teacher well yet, but she is here to help me."

STORIES HEARD AWAY FROM HOME

What negative stories does your mind tell you while you're away from home? Take some time to reflect on a story your mind has recently told you about yourself or the future when you were in a public place. Maybe the story made you feel nervous at a store, restaurant, or park.

What was the story?

- -

- -

- -

What evidence did your mind use to support this story?

- -

- -

- -

What evidence did your mind leave out that could have proven the story wrong?

- -

- -

- -

What would a good friend say to you if they knew your mind was telling you this story?

- -

- -

TALKING TO YOURSELF LIKE A FRIEND

It can be hard to treat yourself kindly when you feel anxious. Anxiety causes your mind to think negatively, which can cause you to be extra hard on yourself. You might say mean things to yourself, for example, "I can't do anything right." This kind of "self-talk"—the way you talk to yourself in your head—isn't helpful. The more harshly you talk to yourself, the worse you will feel.

One way to change mean self-talk is to think about how you talk to people you care about. You probably don't criticize them. You probably give them encouragement by telling them, "You can do it!" or "You're trying your best."

Talking to yourself as you would talk to a good friend is a way to give yourself the encouragement you deserve. It can also help you build courage to handle future mistakes and other life challenges.

Here are some tips to start talking to yourself more like a friend:

→   If you wouldn't say it to a friend, don't say it to yourself.

→   Give yourself the best advice or encouragement you've given to others.

→   Imagine what you'd tell a friend experiencing a situation like yours.

MY NEW MANTRA

A mantra is a motivating phrase you can repeat to yourself when things get hard. Having a mantra ready will help you begin talking to yourself more like a friend. Circle a mantra you could begin using, or write one of your own:

→ "I can practice and do better next time."

→ "Everyone makes mistakes."

→ "I'm trying my best."

→ "I've done hard things before, and I can do them again."

→ "Mistakes help me learn."

→ -

Write your mantra down on a sticky note, and put it next to your bed, on your bathroom mirror, or somewhere else you can easily see it. You will be reminded of your new mantra every day.

GROWTH MINDSET

A mindset is how you see the world. When it comes to you and what you can do, you can have a "growth" or a "fixed" mindset. Having a growth mindset means you believe that you can get better at things with practice. A fixed mindset means you believe you are either good at something or you're not.

People with a growth mindset like learning new things and figuring out solutions to challenges. They don't give up when they make mistakes. Instead, they view mistakes as a way to learn. They keep practicing and improving. Most successful athletes, artists, and musicians have growth mindsets—they weren't born knowing how to do what they're good at. They practiced and became better.

Having a growth mindset is especially helpful for managing anxiety. With a fixed mindset, you might feel powerless, thinking there's nothing you can do when you feel anxious. But with a growth mindset, you believe you can learn new skills to help yourself feel better. It helps you understand that you—not your anxiety—are in charge.

Here are some tips to practice a growth mindset:

→ When something doesn't work the first time, try it in a different way.

→ Add "yet" to your critical thoughts. For example, think to yourself, "I can't figure this out . . . yet."

→ After a mistake, ask yourself what you learned.

→ Reward yourself for trying and practicing new things.

MINDSET QUIZ

Circle the mindset of each thought below.

1. **"I can never do anything right."**

   Growth mindset   Fixed mindset

2. **"I can't figure out this math problem . . . yet."**

   Growth mindset   Fixed mindset

3. **"I'm always going to be terrible at soccer."**

   Growth mindset   Fixed mindset

4. **"If I practice, I can get better, even if I'm not the best player on the team."**

   Growth mindset   Fixed mindset

5. **"I did terribly on this test, but I can study harder next time."**

   Growth mindset   Fixed mindset

6. **"It's not worth it. I'll never be good enough."**

   Growth mindset   Fixed mindset

Answers: 1. Fixed mindset   2. Growth mindset   3. Fixed mindset   4. Growth mindset   5. Growth mindset   6. Fixed mindset

WHAT YOU'VE LEARNED

In this chapter, you learned how mindfulness can help when your mind has anxious thoughts. You did some fun activities to help you respond in different ways to your mind's worries. You practiced watching your thoughts come and go, identified one-sided negative stories, and came up with coping thoughts. You'll use these tools to continue building your mindfulness toolbox.

Before you move on, take a minute to reflect on your mindfulness practice so far.

In this chapter, I learned:

Learning this information is helpful because:

So far, the most helpful idea or exercise for me is:

CHAPTER FOUR

Focusing on Feelings

This chapter is all about using mindfulness to help you manage difficult emotions like anxiety. In this chapter, you'll learn about different human emotions and new ways to handle anxiety when it shows up. You'll do some fun activities to learn healthy ways to express your feelings.

MINDFULLY FEELING

You've read a lot about emotions in this book. Humans have many emotions. Happiness, sadness, anger, and fear are all examples of emotions.

You experience many emotions throughout the day. Some feel good, and others don't. Everyone has had times when they've felt happy and relaxed. Everyone has felt embarrassed, guilty, frustrated, and anxious, too. It's normal to feel all kinds of emotions, positive and negative. Emotions are neither right nor wrong.

Emotions are felt in your mind and body. Some last for just a few seconds, and some last longer. You may feel more than one at a time. You can feel emotions at different intensities. Strong emotions can sometimes overpower or cloud your thoughts.

Mindfulness helps you become more aware of your emotions as they arise. When you pay mindful attention to how you're feeling in the moment, you can notice any uncomfortable emotions—like anxiety—and lower their intensity. This will help you think more clearly about the situation you're in and what you want to do.

EMOTIONS WORD SEARCH

Learning about the different emotions you have is the first step to noticing what you're feeling. How many emotions can you find in the word search below?

Anger
Anxiety
Calm
Curiosity
Embarrassment
Excitement
Fear
Frustration
Guilt
Happiness
Pride
Relaxation
Sadness
Worry

F	X	R	E	L	A	X	A	T	I	O	N	B
R	U	S	A	D	N	E	S	S	N	K	D	Z
U	W	F	I	J	G	U	I	L	T	V	W	O
S	C	O	Q	F	E	P	V	R	Y	U	O	E
T	M	S	E	L	R	W	Y	S	D	F	R	X
R	G	C	U	R	I	O	S	I	T	Y	R	C
A	N	X	I	E	T	Y	H	J	K	L	Y	I
T	Z	H	A	P	P	I	N	E	S	S	X	T
I	C	F	V	R	R	N	M	D	T	Q	W	E
O	A	E	X	T	I	F	V	P	C	A	O	M
N	M	A	V	Y	D	Y	S	B	A	F	R	E
X	I	R	G	N	E	L	K	W	L	O	Q	N
E	M	B	A	R	R	A	S	S	M	E	N	T

NO JUDGMENT

All emotions—positive and negative—are normal and give you clues about what's happening around you. If you've ever tried, you know how hard it is to stop feeling a certain way.

Mindfulness is about accepting all your emotions, not just some of them. There are no good or bad, or right or wrong, emotions. But your mind might judge them as being one or the other. Many people think happiness is a "good" emotion because they feel good when they're happy. They think sadness, fear, and anger are "bad" emotions because they make them feel bad. Just because an emotion feels uncomfortable doesn't mean it's bad. For example, feeling sad when a friend moves away lets you know how important that friend is to you.

By not judging your emotions, you can learn to understand what they are trying to tell you and how to handle them. Here are some ways you can practice mindfully observing your emotions without judging:

→ Instead of good or bad, try to name the emotion you're feeling.

→ Think about the information your emotion is trying to tell you.

→ Remember it's okay to feel all emotions.

Next Time . . .

Today I felt nervous about going to the eye doctor. I hate how scared I feel sometimes. Hating my fear only made me more anxious. When I got to the doctor's office, it felt impossible to go inside. Next time, I'll practice noticing my emotions without judging them.

NOTICING OR JUDGING?

Learning to simply notice but not judge your emotions isn't always easy. With practice, you can get better at knowing when your mind is judging your emotions. Cross out the following statements that are judging. Do your best—remember, there are no grades here.

1. "I feel frustrated when my sister uses my stuff without asking first."

2. "I shouldn't have gotten so angry."

3. "I hate the feeling I get in my stomach when I feel nervous. I wish it would go away."

4. "I'm worried about finishing my project on time."

5. "I hate when I get anxious about my schoolwork."

6. "I feel relaxed when walking my dog."

7. "I don't want to feel nervous at school."

8. "I feel nervous at school."

Answers: The judgment statements to cross out are numbers 2, 3, 5, and 7.

BEING FRIENDS WITH YOUR FEELINGS

When anxiety feels uncomfortable in both your mind and body, it's natural to want to avoid it. But, as you have learned, pushing difficult emotions away doesn't keep them away.

Avoiding anxiety might help you feel better in the moment. But when it comes back, you haven't yet learned how to handle it. The more you fight with your anxious emotions, the stronger they become.

However, if you get to know your emotions, things can get better. Being familiar with your emotions helps you learn how to handle them. Can you think of a time you were so familiar with something that it became easy? Getting familiar with tough emotions can help you move through them more easily and quickly. It might also help you discover they're not as "bad" or scary as you thought.

Anxiety loses its power and fades when you face it. But sitting with anxiety can be tough. Here are some tips to help you get to know your anxiety better:

→ Say hello to anxiety when it shows up. Pretend you're simply riding on the bus together, but anxiety isn't in the driver's seat.

→ Take deep breaths, and notice where you feel it in your body. Remember that discomfort doesn't mean anxiety is hurting you.

→ Time how long the feeling lasts. You might be surprised that feelings come and go faster than you think!

COLD AS ICE—BUT NOT HARMFUL

Anxiety may not be as powerful as you think. This exercise will help you understand how emotions like anxiety can cause discomfort but can't hurt or control you.

Take an ice cube and place it in the palm of your hand. Notice how it feels.

- -

- -

Does it feel uncomfortable or painful? Rate your discomfort or pain on a scale from 1 to 10.

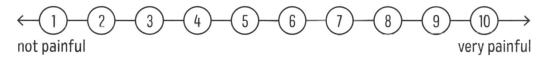

←—(1)—(2)—(3)—(4)—(5)—(6)—(7)—(8)—(9)—(10)—→

not painful   very painful

Do you think the ice cube or the feelings it gives you will last forever?

- -

- -

Did you use any coping skills while doing this activity? How did you sit with your feelings?

- -

- -

WAVES OF EMOTIONS

Emotions are like the waves in the ocean—they come and go. Like waves, they are different sizes and strengths. And also like waves, emotions are always changing. Draw a picture of a beach and a few waves to represent the emotions you've felt today. Draw bigger waves for emotions that felt the strongest or lasted the longest. Draw small waves for shorter and less intense emotions. Label the different emotions that have come and gone throughout your day.

WHERE DID THIS EMOTION COME FROM?

Knowing where your emotions come from is an important step in learning how to handle them. Emotions don't happen randomly. They're usually caused by something.

How you feel depends on what you're doing or thinking about. For example, if your mind is thinking about playing video games with your friends, you might feel happy or excited. But if your mind is worrying about a fight you got into with your friends, you might feel anxious or sad.

Emotions are triggered by things you do, see, hear, smell, taste, or touch. They can also be triggered by certain people or places. For example, you might feel calm while drawing, but you might feel anxious when someone asks you to draw them a picture. You might feel comfortable around your family, but nervous around people new to you.

When you know what triggers your anxiety, you can prepare your mind and body to begin paying mindful attention, or using mindfulness tools, to help yourself feel better before your anxiety becomes overwhelming.

Here are some ways to identify the causes of your emotions:

→ Notice when you feel a change in emotion. What happened right before that change?

→ Are there certain places where you feel less comfortable?

→ Are there certain activities that make you feel anxious?

→ Which people are you most comfortable around? Are there some you aren't comfortable around?

WHAT CAUSES MY EMOTIONS?

Let's get to know some of the causes of your emotions. Fill in the blanks to begin learning about the kinds of activities, people, and places that trigger different emotions in you. The more honest you are when filling out the blanks, the better you will get to know yourself.

This week, I felt happy when I was _. I felt
                                    activity you felt happy doing

nervous or anxious when I was _.
                               activity that made you feel anxious

My friends make me feel _.
                                                          emotion

Being around _ _ _ _ _ _ _ _ _ _ _ _ _ _ makes me feel _ _ _ _ _ _ _ _ _ _ _ _ _ _ _.
              person in your family   emotion

Someone at school who makes me feel _
                                                              emotion

is _.
    name of person

Going to _ makes me feel excited!
                             place

Sometimes, going to _ _ _ _ _ _ _ _ _ _ _ _ _ _ _ makes me feel nervous or anxious.
                              place

Someone whom I feel happy to be around is _ _ _ _ _ _ _ _ _ _ _ _ _, and I feel most
                                            a person you like and trust

relaxed when I'm _.
                           an activity

LET IT OUT

Strong emotions like anxiety can cause a buildup of energy. Nervous energy might cause your mind to have racing or overly critical thoughts. Nervous energy in your body might cause your muscles to tense or your hands to shake or sweat. You don't want to hold onto too much anxious energy because bottling up your emotions can cause them to blow up later in ways that are hard to manage.

Many people release their feelings by talking about how they feel. Talking about your emotions can be a relief—like a heavy weight has been lifted off you. You can talk to a good friend, your parents, a teacher, or any other person you trust and care about.

Expressing your emotions doesn't mean you have to always talk about them, though. You can express your emotions in many ways. You can make artwork or listen to music, for example. You can also express your emotions by writing them down in a journal.

Here are some healthy ways to practice expressing your emotions:

→ Talk to someone you trust.

→ Create a journal, whether on paper or on a computer, and use it to write about your feelings.

→ Get specific about your emotions. For example, if you are happy, think of an even more precise word to describe that feeling.

EXPRESSING YOUR EMOTIONS

Sometimes it's not easy to notice when your emotions are building up. Expressing your emotions every day can be helpful. Pick an activity from the list below, or choose your own, to practice letting out your emotions in healthy and helpful ways. Put a checkmark next to each activity you practice this week.

☐ Talk to a friend, family member, or other person I trust

☐ Write in my journal

☐ Make artwork

☐ Listen to music

☐ Better define my emotions

☐ ---

☐ ---

☐ ---

RESPONDING TO YOUR FEELINGS

Although you can't always control which emotions you feel, you have the power to decide how to respond. Your emotions don't have to control what you do. It might feel like your emotions make you do certain things. But you don't have to do anything your emotions make you feel like doing. You have the final say!

For example, anger might make you feel like yelling or stomping off, but you don't have to. You can choose to do something completely different. You can take a few deep breaths or calmly take a break. Anxiety may make you feel like running away or avoiding a situation. But you can choose to face your fears and show your anxiety that it can't stop you.

Remember, an emotion is just a feeling in your mind and body. It's not an action or what you do. When people do what their emotions make them feel like doing, their lives are being controlled by their emotions. By practicing mindfulness, you can learn how to choose what you do instead of letting your emotions boss you around.

Here are some ways to practice responding to your anxious feelings:

→ Pay attention to what an emotion is telling you to do (for example, anxiety might tell you to run and hide).

→ Do the opposite of what your nervous feeling says (for example, stay still instead of running, or take a small step toward facing your anxiety).

→ Set specific goals that you can work toward so you can stay focused when tough emotions arise.

MY WORRY BOX

Giving your worries a specific time and place can help stop them from taking over your day. For this activity, find a small box or a jar and decorate it. You can use markers, puffy paint, colored paper, ribbons, or any other craft supplies.

At the same time each day, write down any worries, big or small. Fold the slip of paper and put it in your worry box. Now, you don't need to think about this worry anymore until the next day.

The next day, read the worries in your worry box. If you're still have the worry, you can put it back in the box. But if it's no longer a worry of yours, crumple it up and throw it away.

CLASS FACTS

One way to feel calmer when anxiety shows up at school is to mindfully pay attention to what you see. This technique can help you refocus on the present moment and notice just the facts instead of getting caught up in your worries. Focus on describing the people and things near you. Notice any colors, shapes, sizes, textures, and sounds.

Let's practice! Picture a normal day in your classroom. How much detail can you use to describe what you see? Stick to just the facts. Who do you see? How many people are there? What color clothes are they wearing? What shapes do you notice? Do you hear any sounds? At school, you can practice in your head noticing just the facts.

- -

- -

- -

- -

- -

- -

- -

- -

- -

- -

- -

- -

- -

POCKET SENSES

When anxiety strikes in a public place, it can be helpful to have an item in your pocket to focus on. Find a small item that can fit easily in your pocket. It might be a lucky stone, piece of felt, or fidget toy. Place the item in your pocket when you leave your home.

What item will you pick?

- -

When you start to feel anxious, you can refocus your attention on the item in your pocket by using your sense of touch. Practice now.

While taking mindful deep breaths, notice and describe what the item feels like in your hand. Is it smooth? Soft? Bumpy? Describe it below.

- -

- -

Did refocusing your attention help you feel calmer? How does it feel in your body?

- -

- -

Practice this the next time you feel anxious when out in a public place.

FINDING THE GOOD

Anxiety is only one of the many emotions you may feel throughout the day. Anxiety can make you forget about other emotions and the positive things in your life that make you feel good.

One way to bounce back from anxiety is gratitude. Gratitude means being thankful for, and appreciating, the good things in your life. These might include big events like vacations. They can also include everyday events, such as wearing your favorite outfit, spending time with pets, or listening to music.

Gratitude can help you feel better when you've been feeling tough emotions like anxiety. Making gratitude part of your regular routine can add happiness to your life.

Here are some ways to practice gratitude:

→ Make gratitude a habit by practicing it at the same time each day. For example, you could name one thing you're grateful for when you sit with your family for dinner or before you go to bed.

→ Look for opportunities to thank someone for something you appreciate.

→ Keep a gratitude journal. Every day, jot down three good things that happened.

BEING GRATEFUL

Let's start practicing gratitude. These prompts can help you notice good things that happen all around you. There might be many more than you realize! Fill in the blanks.

One good thing that happened to me today was _

_ _

_ _

Something fun that I did today was _

_ _

Today, I smiled when _

_ _

My favorite part of this week is _

Someone I appreciate is _

Something I look forward to is _

_ _

Yesterday, I felt happy when _

_ _

One of my favorite memories is _

_ _

_ _

WHAT YOU'VE LEARNED

In this chapter, you learned how mindfulness can help calm tough emotions like anxiety. You did fun activities to learn about different emotions, your anxiety triggers, and ways to express your emotions in healthy ways. You'll continue using the tools you learned in this chapter as you add to your mindfulness toolbox.

In thIs chapter, I learned:

Learning this information is helpful because:

So far, the most helpful idea or exercise for me is:

CHAPTER FIVE

The Breath and the Body

This chapter is all about using mindfulness to help calm the uncomfortable feelings of anxiety in your body. The activities in this chapter will help you understand how your body reacts when you feel anxious, and you'll learn some new tools to help your body relax.

MINDFULLY BEING

Stress is your body's physical reaction to anxiety. It can show up in many ways. If someone doesn't like flying on planes, for example, their muscles might tense up on the way to the airport. Their hands might feel shaky or sweaty while waiting to board. They might get a headache or feel butterflies in their stomach.

But the feelings you get from anxiety can be the same feelings you get for other reasons that have nothing to do with anxiety. For example, your body also sweats when you exercise. Your stomach may flutter if you're hungry or if you ate something bad.

Mindfulness can help you listen to your body's clues to know which reactions are for which reason. It can help you figure out if a reaction is to anxiety or to other emotions you are feeling. Noticing your physical feelings of stress can help you know if you need to step in to help calm your body before anxiety takes over.

MY BODY MAP

Do you know where and how anxiety shows up in your body? Draw a line to the places where your body might feel each of the following:

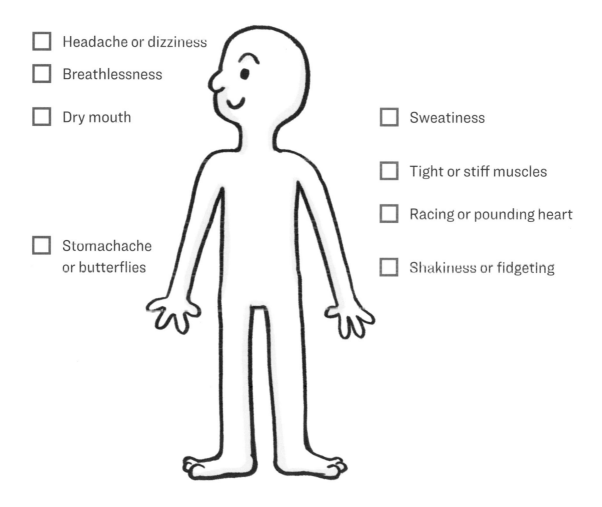

☐ Headache or dizziness

☐ Breathlessness

☐ Dry mouth

☐ Stomachache or butterflies

☐ Sweatiness

☐ Tight or stiff muscles

☐ Racing or pounding heart

☐ Shakiness or fidgeting

Now place a checkmark next to the feelings you experience most often.

RELAX YOUR MUSCLES

These exercises will help you learn how to relax your muscles when they feel tense. In each exercise, pay close attention to how each part of your body feels when it's tense and when it's relaxed. You can do these exercises whenever you notice any tension in your body.

TENSE UP . . .	AND RELAX!
Pretend you're holding your breath under water. Press your lips together tightly to not let any air in or out.	Now pretend you've come up for air. Notice your mouth, jaw, and face muscles relaxing.
Imagine you're a turtle. Gently stick your head out of your shell as far as you can.	Now go back to a regular position. Notice your neck muscles relaxing.
Make a fist and pretend you're squeezing all the juice out of an orange. Squeeze hard!	Now release the imaginary orange. Notice your hand and arm muscles relaxing.
Hold your arms out in front of you and put your hands against a sturdy wall. Pretend to push the wall as far away from you as you can.	Now let your arms drop and hang by your sides. Notice your arms relaxing.
Tighten your stomach by pulling your belly button inward.	Now release it back to its usual position. Notice your stomach muscles relaxing.
Using your toes, pretend you're a monkey gripping a tree branch. Squeeze and hold on tight!	Now release your toes. Notice your feet and leg muscles relaxing.

USING YOUR BREATH

An easy way to practice mindfulness is to pay attention to just one thing: your breathing! Breathing is something that you're always doing. But people hardly ever notice it.

All day long, there are things to distract you. Your mind is bound to wander off, sometimes without you even noticing. You might catch your mind going over something that happened earlier or thinking about something totally random. It's okay—your mind is just doing its job.

Being mindful of your breathing can help give your brain a break from worrying or getting lost in your thoughts. Focusing on what's happening here and now can help you feel more calm, present, and relaxed.

Here are some ways to pay mindful attention to your breathing:

→ See how many breaths you can count breathing in and breathing out.

→ Think about where you feel your breathing in your body. Are you breathing through your nose or your mouth?

→ See if you can notice how other parts of your body move when you're breathing.

Next Time . . .

I was in the school play yesterday. I was nervous about everybody watching me, and when it was my turn to speak, I felt like I couldn't breathe. Next time, I'll refocus my attention on my breathing and take slow, deep breaths to help myself feel calmer.

BELLY BREATHING

Belly breathing is a special kind of deep breathing that helps your body feel calmer by bringing down your heart rate. A slowing heart rate sends a signal to your brain that it's okay for you to relax. Belly breathing strengthens this signal. Here's how to practice this breathing:

1. **Find a comfortable place to lie down.**

2. **Place a stuffed animal, action figure, or other small object on your stomach.**

3. **Take deep breaths, and watch your object move up and down as you breathe in and out.**

4. **Breathe in slowly through your nose. Notice your object moving up as your belly fills with air.**

5. **Breathe out slowly, as if you're blowing air through a small straw. (You can practice breathing out using a real straw if you have one at home.) Notice your object moving down as your belly deflates like a balloon.**

Belly breathing gets easier with practice. Try it for just five minutes a day—even when you're not feeling anxious—so you can do it more naturally when you need it.

STAYING CALM

Many people show their emotions through their facial expressions and body language. Someone who's feeling happy might be smiling. Someone who's angry might have lowered eyebrows or clenched fists.

Sometimes, keeping a calm face and body—even when you're anxious—can help you face challenges. Have you ever heard of the term "poker face"? It describes poker players who show a calm face even when they're feeling different emotions. They don't want other players to know if they're nervous or excited. Famous athletes also use poker faces to show that they're ready to play, even if they're actually anxious about a big game.

You may have used a poker face before to stay calm even when you felt anxious. Maybe you didn't want anyone to know you were afraid to climb a tree. You might have kept a poker face during a party where you felt nervous around new people. Staying calm probably helped you get through and succeed in these tough situations.

Life is full of challenges. Learning how to stay calm under pressure, even when you feel anxious, can help you keep doing the things that you want to do.

Here are some ways to practice mindfully staying calm in stressful situations:

→ Practice belly breaths.

→ Check in with your body and relax tense muscles.

→ Relax your facial expression.

→ Speak slowly and calmly.

MY POKER FACE

Let's see your poker face! Practicing a neutral expression can help you stay calm in tough situations. First, start to calm your mind and body by taking some deep breaths. Then, relax the muscles in your face, including your forehead, eyes, and mouth. Make them as neutral as possible. What does your calm and confident poker face look like? Look in a mirror, then draw it below.

PANIC ATTACKS

Sometimes people say they had a "panic attack" when they felt nervous. But what is a panic attack, really?

It isn't just about feeling nervous. Panic attacks are sudden, powerful physical feelings of anxiety. These might include a pounding heart, sweating, chills, dizziness, or difficulty breathing. They might last for minutes but feel like they last much longer.

Not every one who feels anxious has panic attacks. But people who do might feel like they're losing control. They might even think they're dying.

Panic attacks can be triggered by stressful situations, like having to speak in front of the class. They can also happen unexpectedly without a clear reason.

People who have had a panic attack sometimes worry about having another one. They might avoid places or situations where they think it might happen. Even though panic attacks can feel scary, the good news is you can move through them.

Here are some ways you can get through a panic attack if you have one:

→ Immediately slow your breathing by taking big, deep breaths. This technique can help the panic attack pass more quickly.

→ Move to a quiet space to sit or lie down. Or sit down right where you are.

→ Try relaxing each muscle in your body, going from head to toe.

→ Remember that the panic attack will end.

ACTIVITY 41

PANIC ATTACKS: TRUE OR FALSE

You've just learned what a real panic attack is. Let's see what you know now. Circle whether each of these statements is true or false. (Remember, you won't be graded, so do your best!)

1. **A panic attack is when you feel nervous about something.**

    True   False

2. **Panic attacks are sudden, very strong physical feelings of anxiety.**

    True   False

3. **A panic attack usually lasts for hours.**

    True   False

4. **Everyone who feels anxious has panic attacks.**

    True   False

5. **Sometimes panic attacks can happen for no apparent reason.**

    True   False

6. **You can move through a panic attack if it happens.**

    True   False

Answers: 1. False   2. True   3. False   4. False   5. True   6. True

RESPONDING TO STRESS

Your body's stress reactions are part of human nature. They happen automatically, so you don't always have control over when or how they show up. But you *can* control what you do in these situations. There are many ways to lessen uncomfortable stress feelings in your body.

Many people think they have to do whatever their feelings push them to do. For example, anxious feelings might make you want to run and hide. But you don't *have* to run and hide. You can learn to make decisions and act in ways that are completely different from how you feel inside.

Mindfulness teaches you to know how your body reacts to stress and helps you take control of your actions. When you understand your body's reactions to stress, you can accept them as part of human nature. This helps your physical feelings of stress and anxiety start to feel a little less scary.

BED BODY SCAN

A body scan is a check of each part of your body. It helps you train your attention to notice different body parts and release any tension that you might not otherwise have noticed.

Get comfy on your bed or a couch. Then use this checklist to scan your body.

→ Notice your forehead, eyebrows, nose, and mouth. Relax them if they feel tense.

→ Notice your shoulders, arms, and fingers. Lower your shoulders away from your ears.

→ Notice your stomach rising and falling as you breathe.

→ Notice your legs. Relax your leg muscles and let them fall onto the bed.

→ Notice your feet and toes. Relax and wiggle your toes.

Remember, taking deep breaths can help you focus your attention as you notice each part of your body from head to toe.

FIVE FINGER BREATHING

Five finger breathing is an easy way to practice slowing down your breath when your body feels tense. It can be used anytime, anywhere. Other people probably won't even notice what you're doing.

Using your pointer finger, trace each finger on your other hand up and down. As you trace up a finger, take a deep breath in. Pause for one second when you reach the tip of your finger. Then breathe out as you trace your finger back down. Do this for each finger.

PICTURING MY HAPPY PLACE

People have places they like. Your favorite places are probably those where you have fun or feel happy, calm, and relaxed.

You don't have to actually be in your favorite place to feel good. "Visualizing," or imagining, your favorite place can help you feel better.

Let's try it. Imagine a place that makes you feel happy or calm. It could be a real place you've been to or an imaginary place. Picture it in your mind and focus on as many details as you can. Use your five senses to bring your happy place to life in your mind. Notice what you see there. Can you hear any sounds? What tastes and smells are in your happy place? What can you feel around you?

Draw your happy place in the box. Whenever you feel stressed or anxious, think back to your happy place.

TIPS FOR A HEALTHY BODY

Your body has basic needs—the things it requires every day to stay healthy. Taking care of your body also keeps your mental health in shape so you can manage stress and anxiety. When you forget to take care of your body, you're more likely to be affected by stress.

Two of the most important things your body needs every day are food and water. Your body needs you to eat different types of foods to grow and stay healthy. For example, eating protein and colorful fruits and vegetables gives your body the important nutrients it needs. Drinking water throughout the day keeps you hydrated, energized, and better able to concentrate.

Your body also needs to move every day. Exercise keeps your body working well. It can help you feel physically better and mentally stronger, empowering you to cope with difficult feelings. There are many ways you can move your body each day. You might play sports, do yoga, walk a pet, ride a bike, rollerblade, run at the park, or dance. Even a simple walk around the block is helpful for managing stress.

Like nutritious food and physical movement, sleep is also important every day. Sleep helps your body rest and your mind recharge. It helps you feel refreshed and ready to tackle the next day.

Healthy eating, exercise, and sleep habits lower stress and anxiety.

STAYING ACTIVE

Doing one active thing a day can help you feel less stressed and anxious. Many people find that once they get up and start moving, they begin to enjoy it—even if they didn't feel like doing anything at first. Do your best to commit to doing one active thing each day. Think of your favorite activities that get you moving, then schedule them in the calendar below.

SUNDAY	
MONDAY	
TUESDAY	
WEDNESDAY	
THURSDAY	
FRIDAY	
SATURDAY	

SELF-CARE

Self-care is taking care of yourself so you can feel good and stay strong. It involves all the activities that you do each day to take care of your body and your mind. Taking care of your physical and your mental health each day protects you from stress and anxiety.

It might help to think of self-care as things you do to keep your mind and body's batteries charged. When your batteries are full, you have the power to do your best in life. An empty battery makes doing your best—or doing anything—difficult and sometimes impossible. Self-care activities that keep your batteries charged give you the energy and power to overcome tough situations.

When you practice self-care, you're keeping your life full of positive things that make you feel good. By preventing your batteries from reaching empty, you lower the chances that anxiety will grow too big to handle.

Here are some ways to practice self-care:

→ Try to do at least one active thing each day.

→ Practice mindfulness and relaxation strategies when you're not feeling anxious. Doing so will help you use these strategies when you really need to.

→ Involve some friends and family in your self-care.

MY SELF-CARE PLAN

Self-care is important every day. The key to a healthy plan is to do self-care activities often so that they become part of your everyday routine.

Fill in the following blanks to make your self-care plan.

To take care of my body, I will eat _. I'll stay
healthy food

hydrated by drinking _. I'll stay active by
healthy drink

_ _ _ _ _ _ _ _ _ _ _ _ _ _ and try to get _ _ _ _ _ _ hours of sleep a night.
an active activity   *number*

To take care of my mind, I'll practice _ _ _ _ _ _ _ _ _ _ _ _ _ _ _ _ _ _
a mindfulness or coping tool

a little bit each day. A hobby I enjoy doing or that makes me feel better when I feel

stressed is _.
a fun hobby or activity

I know that I can talk to or hang out with _ _ _ _ _ _ _ _ _ _ _ _ _ _ _
a person I trust

and _.
another person I trust

One activity I'd like to add to my self-care plan is _ _ _ _ _ _ _ _ _ _ _ _ _
another self-care idea

_ _.

WHAT YOU'VE LEARNED

In this chapter, you learned how mindfulness can help you manage physical feelings of stress and anxiety. You practiced some new mindfulness and relaxation exercises, including muscle relaxation, belly breathing, body scanning, and visualization of your happy place. In the next chapter, you'll continue to use these strategies to understand how calming your body can help you take action.

In this chapter, I learned:

Learning this information is helpful because:

So far, the most helpful idea or exercise for me is:

CHAPTER SIX

Taking Action

This final chapter is all about using mindfulness to help you make good decisions and do the things you want to do, even when you feel anxious. You'll learn how people act when they feel anxious, how to make brave moves, and how you can team up with others to get support.

MINDFULLY ACTING

Here's an example of "taking mindful action": Maddie gets nervous talking to people she doesn't know very well. She recently joined a new book club at school, but she has been skipping meetings to avoid talking to people. Maddie starts to really miss reading with the group. She wants to make new friends. She comes up with small steps she can take to rejoin the club. She starts with talking to one friend from the group.

As you've learned, people have a fight-flight-or-freeze response to anxiety. They might cry or yell (fight), run away (flight), or shut down (freeze). These behaviors might be helpful when there's actual danger around, but in everyday situations, they make it hard to do important things.

Maybe you want to visit a friend, but she has a big dog, and your fear of dogs stops you from going to her house. Or maybe you want to go hiking, but your fear of heights stops you. Mindfulness helps you take action against these "fight-flight-or-freeze" behaviors.

Taking action in the face of anxiety might be uncomfortable at first. Mindfulness can help you manage the difficult feelings of anxiety in your mind and body, so that you can make good decisions about how you want to live your life. It can also help you set goals and face your fears, rather than letting anxiety and fight-flight-or-freeze behaviors control what you do.

ACTION VS. ANXIETY

Can you tell the difference between anxious and mindful action? Circle the correct type of action for each scenario.

1.	Staying home from school because you don't want to be called on in class	Mindful action	Anxious action
2.	Raising your hand to answer a question about a topic you like	Mindful action	Anxious action
3.	Asking your parents to order for you at a restaurant because you don't want to talk to someone new	Mindful action	Anxious action
4.	Practicing ordering one item at a restaurant you've been to before	Mindful action	Anxious action
5.	Getting upset when plans changed unexpectedly	Mindful action	Anxious action
6.	Focusing on the present and thinking about what you look forward to in the day	Mindful action	Anxious action

Answers: 1. Anxious action   2. Mindful action   3. Anxious action   4. Mindful action   5. Anxious action   6. Mindful action

SAYING "YES"!

Many people try to make themselves feel better by avoiding things they think will be scary. For example, someone who's afraid of clowns might avoid the circus, or someone who's afraid of swimming might avoid the pool. It's human nature to stay away from things that scare you.

Avoiding what scares you seems to make anxiety go away. It can quickly end uncomfortable feelings like tenseness, shakiness, or sweatiness. You might feel relieved, making you believe that steering clear of a tough situation is the only way to handle it.

But avoiding what scares you actually makes your anxiety come back stronger the next time. When you don't give yourself the opportunity to face your fears, you miss out on learning that you can handle them.

Facing your fears isn't always easy. Here are some tips that can help:

→ Come up with small steps you can take toward your goal.

→ Even if you take no steps, practice staying still in the scary situation and letting your fears come and then pass.

→ Think of situations that used to scare you but no longer do. You are strong!

WHEN ANXIETY MAKES ME SAY "NO"

Understanding what anxiety makes you avoid is the first step to facing your fears. Below are some situations that many kids might avoid when they feel anxious. Check off anything that applies to you and add anything that isn't on this list.

- ☐ Going to new places
- ☐ Going to birthday parties or sleepovers with friends
- ☐ Trying out for a team
- ☐ Trying out for a play or music event at school
- ☐ Talking to adults
- ☐ Talking to kids you don't know well
- ☐ Ordering food at restaurants
- ☐ Sleeping in your own room
- ☐ Raising your hand in class
- ☐ _____
- ☐ _____
- ☐ _____

PARTICIPATING IN YOUR LIFE

The best way to stop your fears from getting in the way of your life is—you guessed it—to face them!

Everyone finds themselves in stressful situations. Mindfulness helps you pause and think about whether fighting, running away, or freezing is necessary. It helps you decide to move toward something that feels scary but isn't actually dangerous. It also makes it easier for you to take brave steps in a new or difficult situation.

Remember, anxiety is part of human nature, so it may not go away completely. The more you practice mindfulness, the more you will see that anxiety can't stop you from doing things you want or need to do. It gets easier each time.

Here are some ways to start practicing taking steps in stressful situations:

→ Plan small challenges for yourself to help you face and overcome your fears.

→ Reward yourself for each step you complete.

→ Be kind to yourself. Anxiety might cause you to continue putting off your goals. Give yourself plenty of opportunities to try them.

→ Ask a friend or an adult for help.

HEART POWER

Let's help you feel more prepared to tackle challenges at home. This exercise will prove your power to calm your mind and body when anxiety strikes at home. Ready to see how?

Here's how to practice:

1. **First, find your pulse. Gently put your index and middle finger on the side of your neck, over your heart, or on the inside of your wrist. You'll know you've found it when you feel some beats.**

2. **Notice the speed of the beats as you're sitting still.**

3. **Do 15 to 20 jumping jacks or sit-ups as fast as you can.**

4. **Find your pulse again and notice any changes.**

5. **Keep your fingers over your pulse and take 5 to 10 deep belly breaths.**

6. **Notice your power to slow down your heartbeat.**

You just proved you can calm your mind and body when you face challenging situations. Practice slowing your pulse with deep breaths. Use these breaths to help calm your body when you face your fears.

MINDFUL ACTIONS

When anxiety arises at school, you might immediately think that you need to avoid what feels scary. Let's practice coming up with more mindful actions you can take instead. For each of these situations, write a mindful action you could take, even when you feel anxious.

ANXIOUS THOUGHT: "I really don't want to play kickball at gym. I might mess up, and my team will think I'm a bad player."

Action I Can Take: _____

_____

ANXIOUS THOUGHT: "I don't want to go to school today because the older kids there will be mean to me."

Action I Can Take: _____

_____

ANXIOUS THOUGHT: "I don't want to do the group project because the other kids won't listen to my ideas."

Action I Can Take: _____

_____

ANXIOUS THOUGHT: "I guess I'll eat lunch alone because no one would want to sit next to me."

Action I Can Take: _____

_____

CLIMBING UP

Think about a goal that anxiety holds you back from accomplishing. We'll break down your goal into steps that will feel doable.

First, write down your goal. It should be something that you would accomplish in a public place—a store, a park, or anywhere away from home.

- -

- -

- -

Now brainstorm three activities related to your goal. For example, if your goal is to try out for the soccer team, some related activities might be playing soccer at home, practicing alone at the park where tryouts will take place, practicing with friends, or talking to the coach.

1. -

- -

2. -

- -

3. -

- -

Write your goal at the top of the ladder on the next page. Write the activities you came up with in order of how anxious they make you feel. Put the easiest activity on the bottom rung and the most difficult one on the top.

To practice facing your fears, do the activity on the bottom rung, then the one on the rung above it and so on. Try to climb all the way up your ladder. Your confidence will grow with each step you take to move closer to your goal.

continued →

Climbing Up, *continued*

GOAL:

3.

2.

1.

CONNECTING WITH OTHERS

Anxiety can make you want to avoid not only situations but also people—especially important people like your friends and family. When you're nervous or anxious, you might not want to talk to anyone. Maybe you don't want others to think badly of you. Or maybe you can't think of the words to explain how you feel.

You don't have to feel alone with your anxiety. Talking to other people when you feel anxious can actually help you feel better. You might be surprised how relieved you feel when you express your worries. Remember that everyone has felt anxious and everyone has had times when they've overcome their worries.

Talking to other people can help you learn new solutions and feel a little less alone with your worries.

Here are some ways to connect with others:

→ Talk to the friends you feel most comfortable talking to about anything.

→ Think of someone who has been successful at doing something you'd like to do. Ask them how they did it.

→ If you feel stuck, pick a trusted adult you think would be happy to talk and listen to you.

CONNECTION SCRIPTS

Sometimes it can be hard to know exactly what to say when you want to connect with others. Here are some things you can say when you want to ask your parents, family members, teachers, or friends.

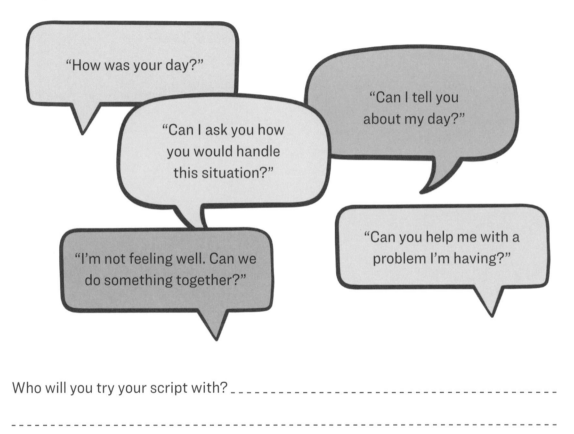

Who will you try your script with? _____

_____

Now, try writing a script on the lines below, where you ask that person for help with something that is on your mind right now.

_____

_____

_____

_____

BEING KIND

Can you think of a time when someone was kind to you and how it made you feel? Maybe a teacher at school asked you just at the right time if you needed help, or a teammate helped you up when you got hurt. Their kindness probably made you feel good.

If you noticed someone wearing a cast, you'd probably offer to help them out. But you can't always see when someone is anxious. Being kind to everyone means you can help others feel good all the time, maybe even when they need it most.

Being kind can also help you feel good about yourself. When you show kindness and help others through stressful situations, you can feel better about helping yourself, too.

Here are some ways you can show kindness and help others:

→ Think of things other people have done to help you and pay their kindness forward by doing those things for others.

→ Imagine how you would feel if you were in another person's situation.

→ Remember not to make judgments or assumptions about what other people are going through.

Next Time . . .

Yesterday, I was rollerblading with my brother. He was skating really slowly and holding us back. Afterward, he told me he was scared. Next time, I'll practice being kind and ask if he needs help.

A HELPING HAND

Remembering times in your life when you've received or given help to others can make kindness a bigger part of your life and reduce stress and anxiety.

Think of a time when someone was kind to you or helped you. What did they do? How did it make you feel?

Now think about a time when you were kind to or helped someone else. What did you do? How did it make you feel?

ASKING FOR HELP

Sometimes, no matter what you do, anxiety feels overpowering. When that happens, remember that you're not alone. You can always ask a trusted adult for help.

A trusted adult is someone like a parent, other family member, teacher, doctor, or other adult who cares about you. It might be someone whom you like to be around or whom you can talk to about anything.

The adults in your life can help when you feel worried. They may have even had similar struggles and can tell you how they overcame their worries. Or they can help you talk to a professional who's trained specifically to help kids with anxiety.

Here are some ways to ask for help:

→ Use your feelings thermometer to measure your anxiety. Ask an adult to help you lower it.

→ If it's hard to say aloud, write a letter.

→ Ask your trusted adult how they would solve a problem.

MY CIRCLE OF TRUST

Let's identify the trusted adults in your life. Think of those who have helped you before. Can you think of someone at home, at school, or in the community to whom you could go for help? Write your name in the middle of the box. Then write the names of your trusted adults all around your name. Now draw a circle around all the names. When you feel stuck, remember your circle of trust.

CONFIDENT YOU!

Confidence means believing you can do something—or at least try it—even when it's scary. It means being brave enough to try and keep trying hard things, even if your first attempt doesn't go well or how you expected. You can show confidence by taking brave steps when you feel anxious.

Confidence can be hard to show in stressful situations, especially when you see other people succeeding. When you're tempted to compare yourself to them, remember that everyone is different and that you have your own unique strengths.

Think back to times you felt confident. Did you attempt something new or challenging and keep trying, even after you made a mistake? Continuing to try new things, even when it feels hard, will boost your confidence.

If you don't have much confidence right now, that's okay. You can build it with practice. The more you challenge yourself to face your fears and do what's important, even when it scares you, the more successful you'll become and the more confident you'll feel.

Here's how you can start building your confidence:

→ Remember your unique strengths. What are the things you're good at?

→ Think about the things that used to be hard but that you find easy now.

→ Set small goals and notice how you feel after meeting them.

→ Take smaller steps even when you feel afraid.

MY BUILDING BLOCKS OF CONFIDENCE

There have probably been many times in your life when you've practiced something and gotten better at it, even when you were scared at first. These experiences are your building blocks of confidence. Jot them down here. Congratulations! Now you can continue building your confidence. Add to this list as you practice and get better at anything.

WHAT YOU'VE LEARNED

In this chapter, you learned how mindfulness can help you make brave decisions and take action when you feel anxious. Throughout this book, you've learned many new tools that can help you handle anxious thoughts and calm feelings of stress in your body. Way to go! As you keep practicing mindfulness, you'll get even better at using it to deal with anxiety.

In this chapter, I learned:

- -

- -

- -

Learning this information is helpful because:

- -

- -

- -

So far, the most helpful idea or exercise for me is:

- -

- -

- -

MORE TO LEARN

BOOKS

Anxiety Relief Book for Kids: Activities to Understand and Overcome Worry, Fear, and Stress by Ehrin Weiss, PhD
> Read this book to learn even more about anxiety and healthy ways to cope with it. Find fun writing, drawing, and other mindfulness activities.

Mindfulness for Kids in 10 Minutes a Day: Simple Exercises to Feel Calm, Focused, and Happy by Maura Bradley
> Try this book's simple meditations and breathing exercises to practice mindfulness in a few minutes a day.

The Mindfulness Journal for Kids: Guided Writing Prompts to Help You Stay Calm, Positive, and Present by Hannah Sherman, LCSW
> Use this journal to write about your mindfulness journey anytime and anywhere.

WEBSITES

The California Healthy Minds, Thriving Kids Project
ChildMind.org/healthyminds/students
> Find videos about mindfulness specifically for elementary school students. Learn more about managing intense emotions, understanding thoughts, and practicing relaxation skills.

Mindful Schools
MindfulSchools.org/free-online-mindfulness-class-for-kids
> Discover 10 free classes to learn about mindfulness and do fun activities.

National Institute of Mental Health
NIMH.NIH.gov/health/publications/get-excited-about-the-brain
    Learn fun facts about the brain and mental health in this free coloring and
    activity book for kids ages 8 to 12.

Nemours KidsHealth
KidsHealth.org/en/kids/center/relax-center.html
    Find a dozen-plus links with help for self-care, managing stress and anxiety at
    school, handling peer pressure and bullies, asking adults for help, and more.

APPS

Headspace for Kids
Headspace.com/meditation/kids
    Discover guided mindfulness meditations and videos to learn more
    about mindfulness.

INDEX

A

Acting mindfully, 108–109, 114
Anxiety
    definition of, 2
    kinds of, 13
    measuring levels of, 3
    mindfulness for, 27
    naming, 14

B

Beginner's attitude, 37–38
Belly breathing, 92
Body
    anxious feelings in, 9–10, 89
    body scan, 98
    healthy needs, 101
    muscle relaxation, 90
Breathing exercises, 30, 91–92, 99

C

Calmness, 93–94
Circle of trust, 122
Confidence, 123–124
Connecting with others, 117–118

D

Deep breathing, 30

E

Emotions
    effects of anxiety on, 11
    expressing, 77–78
    feeling, 68–69
    getting to know, 72
    noticing, 70–71
    responding to, 79
    triggers of, 75–76
    uncomfortable, 73
    waves of, 74
Exercise, 101–102

F

False alarms, 4–5
Fears, facing, 110–112
Feelings thermomotor, 3
Fight-flight-or-freeze response, 4, 9
Five finger breathing, 99
Fixed mindset, 62–63
Food, nutritious, 101

G

Goal-setting, 115–116
Gratitude, 83–84
Grounding exercises, 28
Growth mindset, 62–63
Guiding stars, 17–18

H

Happy place, 100
Heart power exercise, 113
Help, asking for, 121–122

J

Judgments
  of emotions, 70–71
  noticing, 31–33
  of thoughts, 47

K

Kindness to others, 119–120

M

Mantras, 61
Memory game, 26
Mind-body connection, 29
Mindfulness, 22, 25, 27, 39
Mindset, 62–63
Muscle relaxation, 90

P

Panic attacks, 95–96
Poker face, 93–94
Positive attitude, 40
Present moment attention, 23–24, 34–36

R

Refocusing attention, 82

S

School anxiety, 81, 114
Self-care, 103–104
Self-talk, 60
Senses, 28
Storytelling by your anxious mind, 49–52, 59
Strengths, 15–16
Stress, 2, 88, 97, 112

T

Thought experiment, 48
Thoughts
  coping, 53–54, 57–58
  effects of anxiety on, 11–12
  negative, 57–58
  nighttime, 56
  noticing, 44–46
  responding to, 55
Triggers, 6–8, 75–76

W

Watch a movie of your life exercise, 35–36
Worry, 2, 55, 80

Y

"Yes," saying, 110

ACKNOWLEDGMENTS

Thank you to the Callisto Media team for the opportunity to make my dream of writing a book come to life. A special thank you to my editor, Julie Haverkate, and to Maxine Marshall for helping me each step of the way. Mom and Dad, I wouldn't be where or who I am without you. Joe, Kristi, and Ashley, thank you for cheering me on as I wrote my first book. Finally, to the children and parents who have let me into their lives, thank you for your bravery and trust in me, which helps me help others every day. This book is all because of you.

ABOUT THE AUTHOR

 **AMY NASAMRAN, PhD,** is a licensed psychologist who specializes in working with bright young children and their families. She has over 15 years of experience working with neurodivergent and anxious children in schools, hospitals, community centers, and their homes. In her private practice, Dr. Nasamran empowers young children (and their parents), helping them succeed, grow as a team, and become their best selves. Dr. Nasamran is also committed to scientific and evidence-based practices, and contributes to several federally funded research projects to advance mental health care for children and families. She holds three psychology degrees: a bachelor's degree from the University of California, Los Angeles, and master's and doctorate degrees from Michigan State University.